SUM
&ANALYSIS
OF

dare
to
lead

BRAVE WORK.
TOUGH CONVERSATIONS.
WHOLE HEARTS.

A GUIDE TO THE BOOK
BY BRENÉ BROWN

BY ZIPREADS

NOTE: This book is a summary and analysis and is meant as a companion to, not a replacement for, the original book.

Please follow this link to purchase a copy of the original book: https://amzn.to/2Fv6dCc

TABLE OF CONTENTS

SYNOPSIS

In her book *Dare to Lead: Hard Work. Tough Conversations. Whole Hearts.*, Brené Brown explores the power of courage and the strength that can be found in your willingness to embrace vulnerability.

When it comes to shifting culture, improving performance, and finding success, Brown contends that the courage to be vulnerable is at the center of it all. She presents clear strategies that can help you become a more effective leader and better support your team, beginning with understanding the psychology and universal human emotions that cause certain behaviors to manifest.

Drawing on nearly two decades of research on the power of vulnerability and shame, Brown shows you how to embrace your values and strengthen your ethics in order to find authenticity. She encourages you to write your own "story," meaning that you should take charge of the narrative of your own life, altering where necessary in order to be in line with your moral principles.

Dare to Lead isn't just another book about leadership. It is a call to action, one that asks you to be brave enough to show your emotional vulnerability, in order to connect with others on a deeper and more human level.

PART 1: RUMBLING WITH VULNERABILITY

SECTION 1: THE MOMENT AND THE MYTHS

Brown uses a quote by Theodore Roosevelt as the epigraph of the book:

"It is not the critic who counts; not the man who points out how the strong man stumbles, or where the doer of deeds could have done them better. The credit belongs to the man who is actually in the arena, whose face is marred by dust and sweat and blood; who strives valiantly; who errs, who comes short again and again… who at the best knows in the end the triumph of high achievement, and who at the worst, if he fails, at least fails while daring greatly." (Theodore Roosevelt, as cited in Brown, loc. 150).

Throughout this section (and the remainder of the book), Brown frequently refers back to this quote, using it as a north star to guide the reader's journey towards a complete understanding of vulnerability and bravery.

Brown also uses this section to outline some basic *"rumble"* tools. *"Rumbles"* are conversations in which being vulnerable is accepted, encouraged, and even celebrated. Finally, Brown dissects the *"Six Myths of Vulnerability"* that she has come across in her research on vulnerability over the years.

Key Takeaway: Failure is inevitable.

According to Brown, it is important to remember that vulnerability does not necessarily equate to success. On the contrary, it actually takes a good dose of courage to be vulnerable because putting yourself out there means that you will eventually fail at something. This is what Brown calls "*the physics of vulnerability*" (loc. 347).

Brown believes that in order to fully embrace vulnerability you have to be brave even when you cannot control the outcome. She also points out that the Roosevelt quote made her realize that your opinion is only valid if you are actually putting yourself out there too. No one has the right to criticize or judge another's vulnerability unless he or she is open to being vulnerable (and the eventual failure that comes along with it) as well.

Key Takeaway: To love is to be vulnerable.

"To love at all is to be vulnerable. Love anything, and your heart will certainly be wrung and broken. If you want to make sure of keeping it intact, you must give your heart to no one... lock it up safe in the casket or coffin of your selfishness. But in that casket—safe, dark, motionless, airless—it will change. It will not be broken; it will become unbreakable, impenetrable, irredeemable." (C.S. Lewis, as cited in Brown, loc. 381).

Attempting to protect yourself from the discomfort of vulnerability by avoiding feeling emotion robs you not only of painful emotions, but also all positive emotions as well.

When you fear being hurt or heartbroken, you can put up walls to shield yourself. However, these walls will also keep you from experiencing love, which is the essence of vulnerability.

Key Takeaway: Vulnerability is strength, not weakness.

Being courageous implies being open to vulnerability. People often think of vulnerability as being weak, but, paradoxically, it takes great strength to allow your weaknesses to be exposed.

Key Takeaway: Vulnerability is not optional.

Life is filled with uncertainty, and change is inevitable. As you cannot control everything at all times, there will come a time where you will have to be vulnerable, whether you choose to or not. Accepting vulnerability is a sign of maturity.

Equally, we cannot avoid vulnerability by avoiding others or refusing to engage. *"To grow to adulthood… is not to become autonomous and solitary, it's to become the one on whom others can depend"* (John Cacioppo, as cited in Brown, loc. 433). Humans are a social species and, as such, hardwired to seek out connection.

You also cannot avoid the discomfort of vulnerability through engineering. While "systemic" vulnerability can be fatal in industries such as aviation and medicine (and is therefore engineered out of existence in those systems), "relational" vulnerability is still key in those same industries.

Key Takeaway: Trust is earned in small moments.

The relationship between vulnerability and trust can be described as a chicken-and-the-egg type scenario: *"We need to trust to be vulnerable, and we need to be vulnerable in order to build trust"* (loc. 497).

Although trust is often depicted as something that occurs in an all-or-nothing moment, trust is actually something that is slowly built up over time. This principally occurs in small, mundane everyday moments and reciprocal vulnerability. Vulnerability and trust are positively correlated, meaning that they both increase together over time in a relationship.

Key Takeaway: Equip yourself with "rumble tools."

One concrete "rumble tool" outlined in this section is to write down the names of all of the people whose opinions matter to you on a one inch square piece of paper. The key is to identify those individuals who love and support you, and who appreciate your imperfections. The paper is small so that you can really think about whose opinions of you are important.

A second tool is to ask, "What does support from me look like?" This gives others the opportunity to elaborate and give clear examples of the kind of support they need to make a project a success.

A third rumble tool is to say, "Say more." This shifts the focus of the conversation to the other person, allowing for listening and understanding on a deeper level.

Key Takeaway: Vulnerability requires boundaries.

You should be careful to set clear boundaries and to be clear on your expectations and your own intentions before attempting vulnerability. The goal of vulnerability is not to "vent" or "purge" your emotional baggage. It is not to gain sympathy. The goal of vulnerability is to allow yourself to feel (both positive and negative emotions) and to be free to innovate without fear of the inevitable failures that come along with dreaming and creating.

SECTION 2: THE CALL TO COURAGE

In this section, Brown calls her readers to embrace courage using the metaphor of a cave, based on this quote: *"The cave you fear to enter holds the treasure you seek"* (Joseph Campbell, as cited in Brown, loc. 804) Brown shares personal anecdotes illustrating how trust can be built based on honesty and connection.

Key Takeaway: "Clear is kind. Unclear is unkind."

Oftentimes, people fall into the trap of thinking that honesty is too brutal and, therefore, unkind. However, as Brown points out, lying or sugarcoating the truth is actually unkind and unfair to others. Everyone wants to be clear on expectations and to be talked *to* rather than being talked *about*.

Key Takeaway: Give yourself permission to feel is powerful.

Giving yourself the permission to do something vulnerable and to feel is an incredibly useful method to increase accountability.

You might try starting a meeting with each person sharing his or her "permission slip." For example, one person might say, "I give myself permission to stay open to new ideas." This allows you to state your intentions and get the support you need. It also enables teams to increase communication and understanding.

Key Takeaway: Explore simple methods to increase team coherence.

One of the most powerful tools to increase team coherence is as simple as a pad of post-it notes. The procedure Brown calls "Turn and Learn" is simple as well. First, each member of the team takes a post-it and writes his or her estimate of how long a task will take. This can also be used to make list of tasks in priority order.

Then, the group counts to three and reveals their answers. Revealing everyone's answers at the same time is useful because it allows each person to share his or her true opinion without any pressure to conform to group expectations or to what the leader wants.

Key Takeaway: Everyone is responsible for being both optimistic and realistic.

Each individual person should participate in both dreaming and fact checking. You must be able to dream and invent while also staying accountable to reality. *"You must never confuse faith that you will prevail in the end—which you can never afford to lose—with the discipline to confront the most brutal facts of your current reality"* (Admiral Jim Stockdale, as cited in Brown, loc. 877). It is not fair to expect some people to always be dreamers and others to always have to crush those dreams with reality-checks.

Key Takeaway: You are not responsible for other people's feelings.

A key "rumble tool" is to take a break anytime that a conversation shifts from being difficult to being unproductive. It is perfectly acceptable to take a time-out and come back to a topic with a fresh perspective.

In any difficult conversation, you must also recognize that other people are free to feel however they want. You cannot be responsible for other people's emotions. In fact, it is impossible to control the way other people feel while trying to serve them as a daring leader.

SECTION 3: THE ARMORY

Wholeheartedness is a word that Brown describes as being about "integrating" the many different aspects of ourselves so that we can remove our armor and bring out the messy, even ugly parts of our past in order to embrace our whole selves. Wholeheartedness is important because shutting down the vulnerable parts of ourselves only leads to more armor and an erosion of trust.

In this section, Brown breaks down the "armory" that we turn to for self-protection. She accomplishes this by breaking down 16 traits of "Armored Leadership," which she compares trait-by-trait with the 16 traits of "Daring Leadership."

Key Takeaway: Perfectionism is self-destructive.

Many people grow up believing that perfectionism is a road to success. However, Brown refutes that idea, instead laying out how perfectionism is a dangerous belief system that undermines our own accomplishments. She describes perfectionism as an addictive "hustle" that is far from the ideal of striving for excellence.

Instead of being about self-improvement or healthy achievement, perfectionism is totally focused on gaining approval from others. Therefore, perfectionists become slaves to other people's perceptions and the unattainable goal of perfection. This rapidly spirals into a vicious cycle of shame and self-blame.

Key Takeaway: Joy is the most vulnerable human emotion.

It can be tempting go into self-protection mode when you feel vulnerable, and most people feel the most vulnerable when they have something to lose. Joy is an incredibly powerful emotion. Joy means we have something good to lose, and this can lead to a sense of foreboding that can rob of us the celebration that should come along with the joyous occasions we experience in life.

The best way to combat this at work is by practicing gratitude. This means establishing concrete gratitude practices that allow you to share your gratitude with your family or colleagues. It is also fundamentally important to take the time to celebrate your achievements—even when there is much still left to be done.

Key Takeaway: It is impossible to selectively numb emotions.

When you experience negative, difficult emotions, it can be tempting to turn to addictive or numbing behaviors to take the edge off—whether that be alcohol, drugs, comfort eating, sex, TV, staying busy, the Internet, or any other number of crutches people use for instant (but temporary) relief of stress. While these can be healthy in moderation, too much numbing behavior can keep you from feeling positive emotions as well as the negative ones you seek to avoid.

To find healthier and more nourishing ways of coping with difficult emotions, Brown encourages the reader to dig down deep and find the roots of negative feelings. In doing so, you will be able to find a more permanent and supportive solution, rather than a quick fix that leaves you feeling even more empty in the end. It is also pivotal to set clear boundaries that combat the feelings of resentment that can drive people to turn to emotional numbing.

Key Takeaway: Transition from always *knowing* to always *learning*.

In order to shift your perspective and keep "always learning" at the forefront of your leadership skills, you should begin by increasing your curiosity and critical thinking skills. Instead of seeking to have the right answers, you should try to ask the right questions. Additionally, you should reward curiosity, a willingness to learn, and great questions posed by your team.

Key Takeaway: Contribute more than you criticize.

When you criticize without contributing, you are not moving a project or idea forward. Instead, you are stifling creativity and curiosity. You should be cautious of criticism hidden in nostalgia (wanting to stick with the way things have always been done) or what Brown calls "the invisible army" (proceeding as though your criticism represents the majority opinion of a larger group).

To combat the negative effects of criticism, you should be prepared to back up your perspective with a concrete contribution. You must participate and put yourself out there.

Key Takeaway: Daring leaders share context and normalize fear.

True leaders are not afraid to back up their ideas with context or to explain *why* a certain decision was made. They do not fear the truth because they know that people appreciate truthfulness over immediate comfort.

Daring leaders also normalize and speak about fear and uncertainty. While keeping people ignorant and afraid is a powerful tool for social control, it is not courageous or ethical to rule through fear. Instead, daring leaders should acknowledge collective fear and discord without seeking to benefit from the uncertainty that accompanies them.

Key Takeaway: Self-worth cannot be judged through productivity.

Exhaustion has become a cultural norm, but sleep deprivation is an unhealthy trend with many negative health outcomes. You should be intentional about setting aside enough time for a healthy amount of sleep and leisure activities. Business and productivity are not measures of a person's value. Leaders should model healthy behaviors by setting boundaries themselves and demonstrating a healthy work/play balance.

Key Takeaway: Daring leaders acknowledge their own privilege.

The best leaders understand that diversity makes a group stronger because it fosters learning and understanding. They can recognize their own privilege, remain open to learning more about their biases, and understand the responsibility that comes along with their power. They use their authority to support the growth of diversity.

Key Takeaway: Becoming a leader means changing your goals and strategies.

While the majority of people who become leaders got their roles thanks to hard work and plenty of "hustle," the very behaviors that get people promoted are paradoxically the same behaviors that can get in the way of good leadership. Rather than seeking out recognition for him or herself, a strong leader lifts up his or her team and helps the team to shine, not one individual person. This shift in perspective required for strong leadership is not always evident, but it is key to an effective management style.

Key Takeaway: Avoidance behavior is a waste of energy.

When you have to face a difficult situation, it can be tempting to simply flee and avoid the situation entirely. However, dealing with difficult situations is inevitable, and it is much easier to face a difficult problem head-on rather than looking over your shoulder while you run away. Avoidance behavior, such as procrastinating, is therefore a big waste of energy and time.

Key Takeaway: You should aim to lead from *heart*, not a place of *hurt*.

Everyone has experienced hurt in his or her life. Leadership and power are not the places to find control and validation. Instead, you must get to the root of the hurt you have experienced and do the necessary work to heal. This is the only real solution.

Once you have done that, you can use the hurt you have experienced and healed from in order to become a more compassionate leader. Remember that if your management style is based on shame, you cannot ask people to be vulnerable with you.

SECTION 4: SHAME AND EMPATHY

In this section, Brown discusses the relationship between shame and empathy. She asserts that shame is a primal and universal emotion. This means that everyone experiences shame, with the exception of psychopaths, who are incapable of experiencing empathy and human connection. In short, empathy is the antidote to shame.

Brown encourages readers to cultivate empathy in order to break down shame. This is because in order for shame to survive, you have to feel alone. When you speak about shame, it begins to die.

Key Takeaway: Shame is the fear of disconnection.

Shame stems from a fear of feeling disconnection. People are afraid of being misunderstood and/or rejected. In an attempt to protect yourself, you may be tempted to shut down your emotional vulnerability. You may think that you cannot feel disconnected if you do not connect with others. However, paradoxically, refusing to be emotionally vulnerable actually ensures that you will end up feeling disconnection. Not connecting to begin with is just as bad.

Our common humanity is the foundation of empathy. We are all connected in the good and the bad of life. Empathy and the connection underlying it help people to feel like they are not alone in their failures and avoid falling into the trap of shame.

Key Takeaway: Shame should not be confused with guilt or humiliation.

While guilt and humiliation are similar emotions to shame, the difference is that you feel guilty when you think you have *done* something bad. However, when you feel shame you feel like you *are* bad.

Similarly, humiliation is another negative emotion often confused with shame. Usually, you feel that you do not deserve the humiliation you experience. Conversely, shame is felt to be deserved because you feel unworthy of love and connection.

Key Takeaway: Shame is systemic and unavoidable.

There is no such thing as a company that has completely erased shame. The goal is not to get rid of shame entirely as it is so fundamental that this would likely be impossible. The objective is to minimize its effects and to prevent shame from permeating the management and culture to the point that shame becomes the norm.

Remember that control and fear can be used as (destructive) management tools. This should be avoided. It is important to recognize that it is easy to be complicit in a culture of shame when money and power are seen as more important than ethics and values.

While you cannot escape shame completely, you can build up a resistance to shame through empathy. Shame resilience is the ability to face shame without compromising your ethics. When you build up your resilience to shame, you can come out of a shaming experience with increased courage, compassion, and connection.

Key Takeaway: Empathy is about connecting to universal human emotions.

Often, people fear trying to connect with others who are going through difficult experiences they have never personally dealt with. However, unlike sympathy, which is feeling *for* someone, empathy is about feeling *with* someone.

You don't have to have the exact same experience as another person to experience empathy. This is because empathy is tied to universal human emotions such as grief, disappointment, shame, anger, loneliness, and fear. If you have experienced these emotions, you are on your way to emotional literacy.

However, Brown also stresses the importance of recognizing empathy as a vulnerable choice because when you connect with another person's painful emotions, you must also connect with the part of yourself that has experienced those negative emotions in order to feel *with* that person.

Finally, Brown points out that empathy is a skill that must be built up over time. It requires practice and even occasional failure to become truly emotionally literate.

Brown also points out that the biggest empathy pitfall is shaming oneself. When (not if!) you make mistakes, it is important to extend the same kindness and generosity to yourself that you afford to others.

Key Takeaway: You judge in areas where you feel shame.

When you find yourself falling into judgment, this should be a signal to you that the area in question is an area you personally feel shame about. For example, if you judge others based on their appearance, it is likely that you are sensitive to feeling shame in that area of your own life. The problem is that judging others can cause them to experience shame, which can turn into a vicious cycle if they then go on to shame others too.

SECTION 5: CURIORITY AND GROUNDED CONFIDENCE

In this section, Brown discusses grounded confidence, which she describes as *"the messy process of learning and unlearning, practicing and failing, and surviving a few misses"* (Brown, loc. 2353). She presents the following formula for establishing grounded confidence: developing rumble skills, fostering curiosity, and practicing until you get it right.

Key Takeaway: Learning cannot be easy.

Brown points out that when learning is too easy, it is not effective. She explains that learning must activate a desired level of difficulty so that you can feel the mental burn that creates growth, similar to the way that you need to find the right weight to lift at the gym when you want to build strength. In order to build the strong mental skills and self-awareness that underlie grounded confidence, learning and practice must be somewhat effortful.

Key Takeaway: Think more about the problem before you consider the solution.

Einstein one said, *"If I had an hour to solve a problem, I'd spend fifty-five minutes thinking about the problem and five minutes thinking about solutions"* (Albert Einstein, as cited in Brown, loc. 2444). Brown encourages the reader to spend more time understanding a problem before even attempting to find a solution. By expanding your curiosity, you also increase your level of grounded confidence.

Brown also reviews examples of some specific rumble starters she finds helpful when deep-diving into understanding a problem: "I'm curious about," "Tell me more," "Help me understand," "Walk me through," and so on. Each of these phrases heightens the levels of curiosity and communication in your conversations. When you can find common priorities and goals to work towards, you can get on the same page and more easily focus on finding solutions together that move you towards fulfillment of those goals.

PART II: LIVING INTO OUR VALUES

In this part, Brown discusses the concept of living into your values. This involves practicing what you preach—that is to say, putting your values into action. Although courage requires you to set down your amour and be vulnerable, your values and beliefs can help you enter rumbles feeling prepared. Simply put, living into your values means aligning your behaviors with your words, intentions, and thoughts.

Key Takeaway: Values do not shift based on context.

You only have one set of values, which follow you into every context and situation. In order to live into your values, you must be able to put them into words. Brown suggests picking the two values that are the guiding forces in your life. Your values should be so clear in your mind that they no longer feel like a choice, but a natural and immediate reflex that defines who you are. This does not necessarily imply it will be easy, but as Brown points out, integrity means choosing courage over your own comfort.

Key Takeaway: Values need to be operationalized to be teachable.

In order to hold your employees accountable for your values, it is important to teach them those values in a clear manner. In order to operationalize your values, consider the following questions: Which behaviors support your values? Which behaviors are outside of your values? Can you think of an example of a time you fully embodied your values? By coming up with clear examples, you will help to illustrate what your values look like for your employees.

Sharing your values with your team will help you to build trust and connection. Better still, operationalizing your values enables you to be thoughtful and decisive in your decision-making.

Key Takeaway: Daring leaders are not silent about hard issues.

No matter which values are central for you, it is pivotal to recognize the important conversations taking place about privilege, even though they can be very uncomfortable. In order to break through that discomfort, you can start by listening and accepting any criticism that may surface. You do not need to have all of the answers, but a brave leader does not remain silent out of fear.

Key Takeaway: Giving and receiving feedback poses particular challenges.

It can be especially challenging to stay aligned with your values when you are giving and receiving feedback. When giving feedback it is key to be able to recognize the other person's strengths, not just his or her weaknesses. Giving feedback should not only be about criticizing someone's failures, but also about thanking them for their efforts and owning your own part of the situation. You must be able to model the vulnerability you expect from your employees.

When it comes to receiving feedback, you should be able to accept feedback even when the delivery is poor. Being able to take feedback without getting defensive is important because it is the only way to improve over time and eventually achieve greatness.

Key Takeaway: Assume everyone is doing his or her best.

While it is impossible to be sure of someone's intent, an assumption of positive intent means that you operate under the supposition that others are doing their best. This does not mean that you should stop encouraging others' growth. However, you can build respect for what others have actually accomplished, without preconceived ideas of what they *should* be doing.

PART III: BRAVING TRUST

As a social species, trust is a key component in forming deeper relationships and experiencing meaningful human connection. The ironic thing is that everyone wants to be perceived as trustworthy, but most people trust very few others. Braving trust is very important because trust is the glue that holds together teams and organizations and ultimately ensures success.

Key Takeaway: You need to talk *to* people, not *about* them.

When you lack the tool and skills you need to talk directly with people, it is easy to struggle with trust. When you find yourself at a loss for the necessary tools, you risk falling into the trap of talking about people, instead of to them. However, this is a major energy-wasting behavior that is not only inefficient, but can actively break down trust instead of building it.

In addition, when you talk *about* people, the people to whom you are gossiping will also begin to formulate a negative image and see you as untrustworthy. They will start fearing what you might be saying about *them* when they are not around.

Key Takeaway: Asking for help is a sign of strength.

Many people are afraid to ask for help for fear of being perceived as weak or incapable. However, when managers are asked what specific behaviors lead them to trust their team members, the most common answer of what team members can do to earn trust is actually asking for help! This is because the manager is then assured that the person in question will ask for help if he or she needs it, so the manager will not be worried about delegating tasks to him or her.

Key Takeaway: The "BRAVING" inventory helps you get back to the basics of self-trust.

Did you respect your own **B**oundaries? Were you **R**eliable and followed though on your intentions? Did you hold yourself **A**ccountable? Did you honor your "**V**ault" and share information appropriately? Did you practice **I**ntegrity and choose courage over comfort? Did you remain **N**on-judgmental of others and yourself? Were you **G**enerous with yourself?

PART IV: LEARNING TO RISE

In this part, Brown discusses the primordial task of teaching failure. As she points out, it is unfair to ask people to be brave and risk failure if you are not going to teach them what to do if (when!) failures occur. You need to put a plan into place upfront regarding falling and failing.

Key Takeaway: Using specific language is like a neurobiological hack for building up your resilience.

In Brown's research, she found that the most resilient participants all used a version of the sentences: "The story I'm telling myself…" "The story I make up…" and "I make up that…"

When you pretend you do not make up stories, the stories begin to own you. On the other hand, when you take control of your own story, you can rewrite the ending. You own your story, and not the other way around.

Key Takeaway: When you do not have data, there is a temptation to make up stories.

Humans are wired to find patterns by filling in gaps where the information is missing. Neurologists have found that our brains actually reward us for making up a good story, even when it is completely fabricated. You can also be tempted to fill in missing data with your own fears and insecurities and to confabulate by replacing missing information with something you *think* is true but is not.

Key Takeaway: Choosing wholeheartedness is a revolutionary act.

Brown concludes by discussing the revolutionary nature of authenticity and practicing worthiness. She writes, *"Choosing to live and love with our whole hearts is an act of defiance. You're going to confuse, piss off, and terrify lots of people—including yourself... You'll also wonder how you can feel so brave and so afraid at the same time"* (Brown, loc. 3725).

She writes that answering your own personal call to courage and putting down your armor is the first step of daring leadership. In Brown's words, *"The level of collective courage in an organization is the absolute best predictor of that organization's ability to be successful... We fail the minute we let someone else define success for us"* (Brown, loc. 3731).

EDITORIAL REVIEW

In her book *Dare to Lead: Hard Work. Tough Conversations. Whole Hearts.,* Brené Brown digs deep into the paradoxical strength that lies at the heart of vulnerability. Brown contends that the courage to let yourself be vulnerable and embrace daring leadership will revolutionize the way you live, work, and raise your family. She encourages readers to take charge of rewriting their own stories, fully define their values, and connect with others on a human level.

Through a series of personal anecdotes mixed with the findings of two decades of research, as well as case studies of highly successful individuals and organizations, Brown paints a detailed psychological picture of the fundamental human emotions that underlie shame on both the individual and organizational levels. She presents clear strategies to combat shame and to help you become a more effective leader and better support the people around you through empathy, self-awareness, and revolutionary wholeheartedness. Brown's advice is clear and actionable, leaving no doubt as to how readers can put her ideas into practice.

Brown's own authenticity shines through in her writing, and the reader walks away feeling that she walks the walk as much as she talks the talk. Her tone is confident yet friendly, and she is not afraid to use a swear word every now and again. Throughout the book, Brown opens up about her own fears, stubbornness, and failures in her marriage and with her team at work. While these personal anecdotes can at times feel somewhat petty or self-effacing, they do allow the author to strengthen her genuine and relatable voice. The reader truly has the sense that Brown is putting into practice the vulnerability that she preaches, lending the book a clear voice and human perspective.

BACKGROUND ON AUTHOR

Dr. Brené Brown is an American author, speaker, and research professor at the University of Houston. Brown has spent more than two decades extensively studying, writing, and speaking about courage, empathy, shame, and vulnerability. She is perhaps best known for her TED talk, "The Power of Vulnerability," which has more than 35 million views, placing it in the top five most viewed TED talks of all time.

Brown self-published her first book, *Women and Shame*, in 2004. It was later bought by Penguin and republished in 2007 as *I Thought It Was Just Me*. Since then, she has written five more books that have all made it onto the *New York Times* bestsellers list.

Born in San Antonio, Texas in 1965, Brown then moved with her family to New Orleans, Louisiana for a period in her childhood. She subsequently returned to Texas and completed a Bachelor of Social Work (BSW) in 1995 at the University of Texas at Austin. She then completed a Master of Social Work (MSW) in 1996, followed by a PhD in 2002 at the Graduate College of Social Work at the University of Houston, where she now holds the Huffington-Brené Brown Endowed Chair as a research professor.

Prior to completing her higher education and beginning her research career, Brown married her partner, Steve Alley, in 1994. They have been married for almost 25 years and have two children, Ellen and Charlie. Brown resides in Houston, Texas.

OTHER TITLES BY BRENÉ BROWN

I Thought It Was Just Me (but it isn't): Telling the Truth About Perfectionism, Inadequacy, and Power. (2007)

The Gifts of Imperfection: Letting Go of Who We Think We Should Be and Embracing Who We Are. (2010)

Daring Greatly: How the Courage to Be Vulnerable Transforms the Way We Live, Love, Parent, and Lead. (2012)

Rising Strong: The Reckoning. The Rumble. The Revolution. (2015)

Braving the Wilderness: The Quest for True Belonging and the Courage to Stand Alone. (2017)

END OF BOOK SUMMARY

*If you enjoyed this **ZIP Reads** publication, we encourage you to purchase a copy of the original book.*

We'd also love an honest review on Amazon.com!

Want ***FREE*** book summaries delivered weekly? Sign up for our email list and get notified of all our new releases, free promos, and $0.99 deals!

No spam, just books.

Sign up at <u>http://zipreads.co</u>

Made in the USA
San Bernardino, CA
22 February 2019